SIJO CHUNGATH

2012

– Published by the Rev. Dr. Ashish Amos of the Indian Society for Promoting Christian Knowledge (ISPCK), Post Box 1585, 1654 Madarsa Road, Kashmere Gate, Delhi-110006.

© Author, 2012

All rights reserved. No part of this book may be reproduced or transmitted in any form or by any means, electronic, mechanical, photocopying, recording, or by any information storage and retrieval system, without the prior permission in writing from the publisher.

The views expressed in the book are those of the contributors and the publisher takes no responsibility for any of the statements.

ISBN : 978-81-8465-240-6

Laser typeset by
ISPCK, Post Box 1585, 1654, Madarsa Road, Kashmere Gate, Delhi-110006.
Tel: 23866322/23
e-mail: *ashish@ispck.org.in* • *ella@ispck.org.in*
website: *www.ispck.org.in*

Dedication
To my ever loving You

Appreciations

I find the poems of "Celebrations with Heart", simple, deep and thought provoking. Every poem is born out of experience of life, nature and divine. I appreciate the texture and quality of the fabric of these reflective poems. I wish and pray that the spirit of these poems touch our lives and add newness to celebrate life in its fullness.

Mary James mcj

My friend Sijo, in his real life too, is somewhat romantic to nature. The poems of "Celebration with heart" are some waves from his poetic mind through which he reveals some realities of life, of "Mother nature." I really wonder how he could attain such a poetical potential and beauty of alliterations even at this young age. I truly wish and pray that the Lord may fill his life with abundant anointing.

Mini Thattil

Sijo Chungath is my good friend, beyond that when I stand as a person in this world, the author is a 'Poet of Hope' for humanity. Each poem is like a wake up bell to the hearts and minds of the readers and calls for creative change. His poems blend the realms of morality, spirituality, phenomenology, epistemology, metaphysics, anthropology, and contemplative theology. I feel these poems have immense capability to relate the reader to the reality of life, to the world and ultimately to the Creator.

Freejo Chiriyankandath

These fifty verses of "Celebrations with heart" are absolutely lovely, worth reflecting to make life a real celebration, to face challenges optimistically. And with good reason... Sijo always finds beauty and inspiration in everything and his deepest thoughts are best expressed through his poetry. Truly inspiring...

Lindsie Arulkumar

"Celebrations with Heart" springing from the heart of my friend Sijo Chungath delights and challenges the reader with its romantic treatment of nature and optimistic outlook towards life. The clarion call of duty to build a new world and the invariable yearning of the human soul for the

Appreciations

Almighty are the other predilections of the author which make the poems suitable for all the ages and for all.

Anish Jeberson

Fabulous work! Your thoughts, words and creativity, are really incredible. The magical verses of these poems will really touch everyone's heart. The beautiful description of life, earth and nature, God's great handiwork, which have been expressed in these poems, makes me say only one thing, "God has gifted you." Best wishes...

Rajeena Jimmy

The new book of Sijo Chungath, "Celebration with heart", brings different moods of nature and human life and transcends the mind from the empirical realm to the divine. Every poem instills within us the music of nature, reality of life and hope of tomorrow. It is really exciting and exhilarating.

Rijo J. Vadakekudiparayil

*The best and most beautiful things
in the world
cannot be seen or even touched.
They must be felt with heart.*
Helen Keller

Contents

Dedication		*v*
Appreciations		*vii*
Acknowledgements		*xv*
1.	A Fairy Tale	... 2
2.	Delightful Countryside	... 4
3.	The Bounteous Gifts	... 6
4.	The Evening Bells	... 8
5.	You are My Son	... 10
6.	Away from the Crowd	... 12
7.	The Unique Composition	... 14
8.	Remind me Often	... 16
9.	The Eyes of Wonder	... 18
10.	An Uninvited Guest	... 20
11.	When the Days Roll	... 22

12.	Eternal Fragrance	...	24
13.	I have Lived not to the Full	...	26
14.	O! How much Good	...	28
15.	Promise of Life's Destiny	...	30
16.	Long for a Morn	...	32
17.	A Bird up on Skies	...	34
18.	Something Deep to Hope for	...	36
19.	To Become One in Unity	...	38
20.	The Aching Void	...	40
21.	Still less Realized	...	42
22.	Re–Create a New You	...	44
23.	Happiness that Persists Long	...	46
24.	A Real Celebration	...	48
25.	The Greatest Victor	...	50
26.	If You can Dream Still	...	52
27.	White Lilies of September	...	54
28.	Keep Believing	...	56
29.	An Angel from Above	...	58
30.	Time-Present	...	60
31.	An Equivalent Benefit	...	62

Contents

32.	To Beat the Song of Gratitude	...	64
33.	I Need You Now	...	66
34.	Graceful Living	...	68
35.	Freedom ever be with You	...	70
36.	Sacred Solitude	...	72
37.	A Rapture on a Blade of Grass	...	74
38.	Pain and Suffering	...	76
39.	I Meet You Inside	...	78
40.	The Day is not Far	...	80
41.	To Sail Beyond the Sunset	...	82
42.	Roses of a Shy November	...	84
43.	A Search for Identity	...	86
44.	The Breezeless Summer Night	...	88
45.	In the Company of Nature	...	90
46.	The Bond of Life	...	92
47.	The Most Precious Given	...	94
48.	Solemn Loneliness	...	96
49.	A Breeze can Sing More	...	98
50.	Life is to Advance	...	100

Acknowledgements

More than poems in the strict sense, these are hymns of celebrations, born from the encounter of my heart with the realities – God, fellowmen and nature; from the deepest feelings ever cherished in my life's journey. I humbly wish that some with more extensive mind and enlightened mind could have penned them. But here they are, with many imperfections, the fragile shadow of a shining fact.

At this juncture, let me acknowledge gratefully the people who graciously helped me in one way or other in this attempt. I express my profound gratitude to His Excellency Rt. Rev. Dr. Anthony Chirayath, Bishop of Sagar for his appreciation and support. My sincere thanks to Rev. Dr. Devamitra for his encouragement; to Brs. Kiran Olakkengil, Josy Valiaveettil and Liby Puthenveettil for editing and designing; to Feji P. Varghese for adding music notations; to Srs Jessy FCC and Bina FCC for their valuable suggestions and to all who inspired and influenced me in various ways in completion of "Celebrations with heart".

Celebrations with Heart

1
A Fairy Tale

A Fairy Tale

'Life' on planet Earth is a fairy tale:
Once, told among the angels in gale,
Of a wonderful land of odds and colours
Creatures of copious kinds and manners.
The king Sun with his golden gleam,
And his warriors - the stars with beam;
His crown - the bow with seven lining,
His commands in thunder and lightening.
Silver Moon the queen dearest,
With their children lived the longest.

The Planet Earth was their mighty palace
And the courtyard the sky limitless.
Clouds, the messengers in white garments,
To receive the guests - the seasonal winds.
Deep blue oceans to bathe solemnly,
And to take rest mountain and valley.
Rivulets flow ever singing in the garden,
Where the green forests to fresh and warden.
Human beings, their offsprings blessed,
Stayed happily together, always rejoiced.

And those angels even wished to be born,
As humans on this Earth to live on.

2
Delightful Countryside

Delightful Countryside

Delightful, yellow-ripened countryside,
A fresh granary for the world outside;
Autumn fields in their sumptuous dance,
In the ever soothing mountain breeze.

The golden crown and glowing halo,
When the day light gleams getting shallow;
The chirping birds and strutting peacocks,
When the rivulet sings between the rocks.

People of content faces and smiling hearts,
After the long days of their sweats.
In rhythmic steps of harvest song,
And entire nature in grandeur along.

The lining carts with their chiming bell,
Along the muddy paths, they travel;
Hills and steeps, planes and pits all alike,
For their heart with nature is not unlike.

Young or old, bud or wood in chorus,
To celebrate the mood of festal splendiferous;
Gain or loss, tear or laughter but together
The 'goodness' is in sharing all with another.

3

The Bounteous Gifts

The Bounteous Gifts

When I asked for a pretty flower,
For its refreshing fragrance and colour,
I was given an autumn vigour.

When I asked for a ray of light,
For its vital shine to dispel night,
I was given a sun with might.

When I asked for water, a handful;
For its refreshing taste life-full,
I was given a rain plentiful.

When I asked for a friend to share,
For his consoling words as from lyre,
I was given a humanity who care.

When I asked for a day still more,
For its discerning wisdom and lore
I was given again a life-shore.

Lo! How much more is the bounteous given,
In spite of my unworthy soul, greed driven;
When I'll stop my wants, and live the Heaven?

4
The Evening Bells

The Evening Bells

The evening bells of the pagoda, far hill side
Echoes the knell of my life's eventide;
In the temple, erected within by life's ways,
Before the twilight after my colourful days.

The trumpet beats and their thrilling sounds,
And the hands clapped on the victory grounds
Faded and fallen into the trenches of past;
Where the memories struggle to reminisce the last.

The name and fame - the possessions futile,
To lose their form as mountain fog fragile.
Health and wealth, the greatest ever treasure
Also withstand not for long, the time's crusher.

But about the deeds of love, I am undoubted,
That the time devoted for my neighbour is counted.
And values to hold firm make life worth,
Not the monuments of moments build on earth.

And I will wait on the shore for the last combatant,
To hand over my life's record sheet with content.
And to embark to another shore of sacred hymns,
Where there are no evenings and their chimes.

5

You are My Son

You are My Son

How great is your love my Lord
To forgive my depravity;
As an ocean, the mercy you offered
To blot out my malignity.

To come your closer, the grace no more
I turned against you, my face;
As the waves to its favourite shore,
Yet you came to embrace.

Though I floated in the darkness strangely,
You extended warm care;
As the strewed clouds are illumined softly
By the rising sun's glare.

In the lonely planes, when I went to hover,
You accompanied silently;
As the appeasing west wind pats over
Tender wheat stalks gently.

Who I am to deserve all the favours,
Of unworthy life mere?
And wept bitterly when I heard you converse-
"You are my son dear".

6
Away from the Crowd

Away from the Crowd

I have a home away from the crowd,
On the lap of a sacred hillside, hallowed.

Dried hatching grass and palm leaves roofed,
Above the half baked bricks, loosely packed.

O'er and far from fen, moor and morass
A piece of earth, really the gift of a goddess.

The magnificent peacock's dance is not rare,
Among the decorated flora and thick tare.

The silver stream's humming sound in setting,
To the melodious song of cuckoos' repeating.

The assiduous bees from morn till evening,
Express the joy of a harvest by buzzing.

The captivating scent of those wild lilies,
Re-live the sweet but forgotten memories.

In the solemn silence, the majestic mountain,
Watch over the air of peace to remain.

It is really to feel the heaven's miniature
Abundant with the blessings of Mother Nature.

7
The Unique Composition

The Unique Composition

When I reach out fathomless to my core
To the variegated construction to be bore;
A mystery unveiled seldom and the least,
The most near but remain the furthest.
The unity of immaterial elements mattered
And a bundle of contradictions scattered;
I wonder, how I can still sort out-
Into a single peerless person throughout!
Amidst a thousand fluttering thought patterns
And those constant flickering reasons;
Thrown between ups and downs of consciousness,
Savage knacks and countless creativeness.
Seconds to bring various sensations in train,
Spaces to create their imaginations and strain.
Numerous, the looming desires and wants
And the lingering longing for grants;
Also, the pleasing temporal emotions
And their highly seductive passions.
How should I poise my existent being,
Amongst these molten flux ever living?
Would I find a point of saturation,
Over the waves of ever altercation?
Or, do they mould an outside mantle-
The unique composition – 'I' to settle?

8
Remind me Often

Remind me Often

Remind me often my place in the world,
Let me grow in your nature bold.

May I not forget the space around
And be absorbed in self-created round.

May my thoughts not constrict my kind
And shrink into the walls of own mind.

Remind me often the hour of my life,
Let me live worthwhile the present strife.

May I not be lost in the comforts fleeting
And depart from the duties ever lasting.

May my life not ever lament my lot
And forbid to thank for what all I got.

Remind me often my purpose in your plot,
Let me strive hard the plan to carry out.
May I not blind myself, by my ego
And fail to see my neighbour and forego.

May my acts not hurt any least one
And restrict to reach out to your poor one.

9
The Eyes of Wonder

The Eyes of Wonder

Never I ask for these rueful days to move,
Neither a heaven above;
Never I ask for a miracle to take place,
Nor a shower of grace.

Never I ask for a life, full of happiness,
Neither to give the richness;
Never I ask for the comforts ever pleasing,
Nor to live without suffering.

But my Lord, only the eyes of 'wonder'
To look at your splendour,
That to see 'miracles' in everyday business,
Too often drifted nameless.

For the real beauty ever passed unperceived,
And their joy unlived;
For the gifts beginning from umbilical cord,
Countless but perjured.

The kind of wonder to feel good in creation,
To glimpse your manifestation;
And to set my feet on the rungs ascending,
Towards you, All-Pervading.

10
An Uninvited Guest

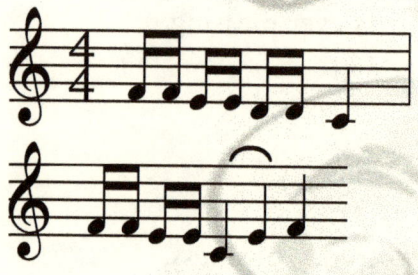

An Uninvited Guest

When you grab sleep from my coach,
Entering through half-closed window of porch

As an uninvited gust of early hour-
The glimmering rays, the bright sun's power.

A reflection of divine halo from above
On the creation, out of overflowing love:

To renew the face of the Earth beloved
The dismay of night, that to be removed.

A clarion call for duty is well conveyed,
And a spring of joy to work accompanied:

To give up the slumber of the last night
To awake, arise and arrest the new height.

I heard you whisper, "Good morning"!
And the greeting of a bright day awaiting:

To replenish life and its very splendour
Dispensing ever the darkness and thunder.

A gratuitous invitation bestowed as treasure
To explore new opportunities, the day to offer.

11
When the Days Roll

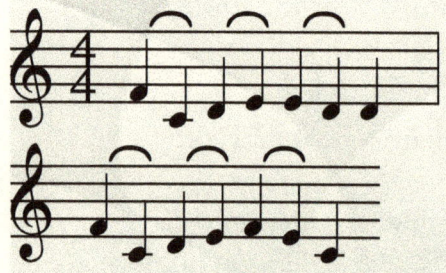

When the Days Roll

When the days roll the time wheel,
The comforts of youth rise appeal
To make you stand outside the way,
For your hair has set out to gray.

Your sound appease the men no more,
Nor strength can bring fame anymore;
Victories have closed the door for ever,
And the days of glories can rise never.

Your eyes start betraying the colours,
And the ears to miss the timbres.
The outer charm is stolen by the days,
As the days are dried by fiery rays.

The ball and wine again, never enjoy,
Nor the baths or bays gift the joy.
The sights you craved, turn to be bored;
Within the people loved, feel to be odd.

Nothing of the world is devoid of change
For a dawn, its dusk is not strange.
Look into the soul which never decay,
The treasure that ever not go astray.

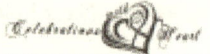

12
Eternal Fragrance

Eternal Fragrance

Beauty is eternal fragrance of perception,
In spite of the difference in conception.
For, simple or composite, odd or set manifest-
The craftsmanship of the Greatest Artist.
The less good is only that less perceived,
For the goodness is never fully conceived.
As the ocean water can be ever vapourized
By the heat of a sun fully energized.
The world is vivid, novel and magnificent
Even much not we apprehend.
Its beauty remains ever a mystery,
Though the manifolds come and go in history.
The wild daisy left unperceived,
And the pebbles of the riverside unnoticed;
The tender leaves of the tall palm trees,
The components of a mountain breeze,
All partakes in the same beauty infinite;
As the rays emanate from the same light.
Even shared in the countless variety,
Beauty remains ever same in intensity.
Behold! It is here, around and everywhere,
In this starry night's silent stare.
Also in the rose garden, outside window pane;
More than, within your radiant heart's plane.
"I have lived not life to the full"

13

I have Lived not to the Full

I have Lived not to the Full

The pale leaf solicited to the cold wind;
Trembling and shivering, all distressful
In the forthcoming fate with wavering mind.

Just a day more with the dear ones:
To say goodbye to the stem and roots,
To remind the fall inevitable to other ones;
Not to be proud of vital green shoots.

West wind was too busy to hear the pray
And passed along with its buzzing voice;
Shaking the branches, raising the hay,
As a merciless combatant of a war place.

The little leaf was gushed out to wilderness
In the evening of its life and the day;
Slowly and slowly fluttering in vastness,
Touched the ground insecure and gray.

The stories of thousands fallen before
And the whisper of nights made her bold;
The fear was eloped and she waited for:
The day to be one with Mother Soil fold.

14

O! How much Good

O! How much Good

O! How much good, it is to be in love,
To be loved and to love all above.

Every moment passing and awaits it means,
How different, special, novel the scenes.

The tears turn sweet and tender the joy,
Nothing on the earth or above to annoy.

How rich the silence and beautiful the night,
Even the dark has nothing to hide from sight.

The day stops never, bringing the surprise,
As a dawn forgets never to bring the sunrise.

Lo! The birds' chirping turned a new song
And the winds' whistling its music along.

So charming now the shades of wayside;
How ardent the air now entering inside.
Passionate musings rise above the heaven,
Delightful dreams decorate the bow of seven.

O! How good is now the world all around,
How much the feeling, love could surround!

15
Promise of Life's Destiny

Promise of Life's Destiny

Death is only once for the brave,
Those who destined to live the full.
For it's not a process, lead to grave,
But a reward of a life, mindful.

In death the meaning of life is carved,
For the struggles, strains and changes.
It is the privilege of only who lived,
The one who stood over its challenges.

Death is a passing of acts to ideal;
As a melody of flute diffuse in nature,
As a candle burns out leaving its material
To dissolve in air, the vast stature.

It reminds the value of this very life
Not as a possession, but as a gift limited.
A motive to perform the duties and strife,
To set before the call, undoubted.

It's not a loss, but an act succeeding,
Towards a world of better harmony;
Also not an end but an opening,
To achieve the promise of life's destiny.

16
Long for a Morn

Long for a Morn

I long for a morn again
A bright dawn to dispel the shadows of dullness;
For, I wander so long among the shades lifeless.

I long for a morn again
To wake from the sloth of a slumberest night,
And to act the duties of the day with might.

I long for a morn again
For, the darkness deepens in and around the room,
And makes me sink amid the encircling gloom.

I long for a morn again
Real rays of wisdom to discern the truthfulness;
For, I am lost among the scales of worldliness.

I long for a morn again
A watchful heart to preserve the day's goodness-
Against the sullen days' creeping grayness.

I long for a morn again
To experience a world with colours and variety,
Over the dull hours of night's depravity.

I long for a morn again
To receive the warm wind of hope and desire,
Instead the night's cold wave of death and despair.

17
A Bird up on Skies

A Bird up on Skies

I would rather be a bird up on skies,
If a birth I was offered again.
For the wings would take me the highs
O'er the clouds, in touch with the divine.

Away from the clutches of noisy place,
Far from the sights of madding crowd;
In solace and peace prevailing space,
Musing long on your greatness loud.

Frisking with the refreshing haze,
Above the proud mountain peak.
A life not tensed with passing days,
And the temporal wealth to seek.

Floating soft in the soothing breeze,
To enjoy the freedom after the horizons.
The limitless air to breathe and appease,
Over the unnatural human confines.

It's a leap, still to uncertainty,
From the comforts of a secure nest.
But I find it as acute necessity
To rise above, till I meet the quest.

18

Something Deep to Hope for

Something Deep to Hope for

Something deep to hope for in life,
A wish not fulfilled, yet to strife.
It is the fuel to burn my lamp,
And to roll the wheel without damp.

It keeps a new morrow awaiting,
A dawn with new light enchanting;
Thinking of the time that favours,
To bloom my life with odours.

A change to keep the desire aglow,
To move from the peripheral shallow.
A hunger to crave for the more,
To know the real that we adore.

To go beyond the appearances,
To look beneath the surfaces ,
To know more intricate intimations,
To reveal the hidden manifestations.

For I know the restlessness remain,
As an image departed from genuine;
Until I climb the ladder of wonder,
To reach to a world above the thunder.

19

To Become One in Unity

To Become One in Unity

A moment is sufficient for realization:
There is no margin of differentiation,
That your uniqueness is not a contradiction
To separate from the entire extension.
The dichotomy is only a fleeting illusion
And disappear in the right comprehension.
You are in 'nature' and part of its cosmosity,
Also 'you' contain a nature in its veracity.
You think, walk, learn, act in nature;
Without nature you can never nurture.
For, you carry a nature within, every time,
The face which is revealed in mime:
The wide skies and the stars shining,
The deep seas and the waves lining;
The morning sun's refreshing brightness,
And winter wind's freezing numbness;
A butterfly's designed colour distribution,
Blooming bud's myriad petal construction.
Nothing in nature stands outside your inside,
And yet in this vast variety you reside.
At the moment you conceive real awareness,
And stand rapt in mysterious extensiveness,
You'll feel that you are dissolving in parity
In her body to become one in unity.

20

The Aching Void

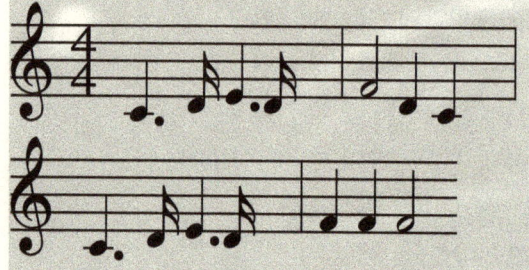

The Aching Void

The aching void of my heart endless,
To be filled by you my Lord;
The painful longing of my soul timeless,
To be touched by you my God.

For a brittle earthen lamp for long I am,
Without the oil of life to burn.
Waiting so long for your breath warm,
The lost soul's exuberance to return.

For I am a harp derelict and uncared,
With broken strings and empty notes;
Lingering for my master's touch powered,
To bring out a melody of praise denotes.

Fill me Lord; only you can fill the void;
You can quench the thirst of my soul.
Your single breath can grant the fire devoid,
To shine for the ages yet to roll.

Touch me Lord; you can pitch the number;
Only you can tone the strayed plays.
Your single touch will break the slumber,
To sing your wonders all the days.

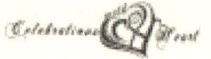

21
Still less Realized

Still less Realized

This world is still less realized
Because, often the real our eyes refused.
We hooked on the glittering pleasing
And left out the irksome facts causing.
Decorated mansions and skyscraper monuments,
Dammed our sights from muddy pavements;
Material comforts and new-age pleasure,
Kept us away from valid exposure.
The face of earth is not so white-washed,
Nor her sons are living all polished.
Truths are all bitter, naked in bluntly,
But we dilute to digest them easily.
The hungry children and their empty belly,
The shivering hands, the numbness deadly;
The cry of the homeless and yawn of jobless,
The grave fate of the large but voiceless.
We dump ourselves or pretend as not seen,
Or as they are not the part of the world scene;
And still brood over another want to hatch
For, the new values permit the right to snatch.

When we would reach a stage of realization,
To limit our desires and to feel saturation?
When our eyes would perceive the reality,
To act human and to feel with human?

22

Re-Create a New You

Re-Create a New You

Lo! The grace of this moment,
Leave not without feeling the fervent;
For, every second is different and novel
In its richness, ever marvel.
Behold! It's new air in every breathing,
And a new ray encountering.
It is the new sun to witness,
And a new art in sky's vastness.
Descry! It's a new breeze to welcome
And a new face, to overcome.
Discern! It's a new heart-beat
And a new sensation, inside to meet.
For every moment brings a new possibility-
To invest your creativity;
And carries always new challenges,
To demand the new changes.
For, every hour has its call for duty,
To make a new humanity.
And still...
Are you the same?
Awake, chop and change;
Fathom, the accountability in every stage.
Adhere to the moment given,
To re-create a new 'You', spirit-driven.

23

Happiness that Persists Long

Happiness that Persists Long

Real happiness that ever persists long
Is not in pleasure's fleeting song;
Also not in the costly costume's line
Nor even in a day's delicious dine.

For money cannot purchase a smile,
If you are not happy within a while;
Nor the material comforts can confer,
If your heart has no content to offer.

The deeds done for self-glory in vain
The ears tuned for the praises main;
Never you meet within true happiness,
Unless start searching other's gladness.

Happiness you receive, only by giving
In the deeds of all self-emptying;
In the sacrifice of a meal to the poor,
In offering what you own, to the weaker.

In extending your hand to the destitute,
In listening to the sorrows of the desolate,
For, happiness is a gift tagged together
In becoming human, by loving another.

24
A Real Celebration

A Real Celebration

The life on earth, a real celebration,
From birth till death around all together;
Where you are immersed in vast creation,
Wonders after wonders always to gather.

In the songs of Mother Nature melodic,
Thousand colours flowered in the lap;
In the blessings showered in rain sonic,
The charming bow bloomed to swap.

The more we know the more we celebrate,
For life is to love the joys of varied kinds.
Everything is novel, splendid and delicate,
For we come with empty hands and minds.
Every night to cradle joyful longings,
And every dawn a herald of new hope,
Every event to bring forth plentiful crop,
To celebrate a harvest of sweet feelings.

Every season to gift a new fragrance,
And every full moon, a new dream;
One and all around to add the refulgence
To this life of ever joyous stream.

25

The Greatest Victor

The Greatest Victor

I met him in a waning dusk-
Proceeding to the West with the sun;
Strange in his looks as an alien
But, grace in his face as a prophet.
It was not an evening in his eyes
Instead, the rays of a summer dawn;
The saffron fringes fluttered in the wind
But, ever not his steadfast mind.
The long disciplined hair highlighted-
The uncommon elegance of his expression.
His hands were empty, body half naked,
But the face reflected the highest king.
Nothing to be felt lacking in him,
Walking bare foot, yet majestically.
He spoke nothing on the way-side,
Yet everyone heard a call, deep inside.
Besides, he asked not anything about
But, the ways of lives were questioned.

And he fainted from my eye-sight,
Making me to think still further:
Who is the greatest or a real victor?
The one who conquered the world or the self?

26

If You can Dream Still

If You can Dream Still

If you can dream still,
You are defeated not yet;
A dawn awaits, ahead the set.

Sun, gift of the East,
Never fails to heed the wishes-
To accord the colours in splashes.

A will to give the sweat,
Can yield bone and flesh;
Whatever may be your wish.

If you dare to touch the star,
The bow will bridge the stretch
Or night will bring her to the reach.

The worst will turn to the best,
When you start to strain
Investing the heart over pain.

Only that day will be yours,
Where you lived right its moments
And added your life's fragrance.

27

White Lilies of September

White Lilies of September

White lilies of serene September,
After a long ransom rain;
The most graceful gift of the Creator,
As a reward of the Earth's pain.

The most fascinating in shape and scent,
Yet simple and humble in nature.
How gentle, charming and fervent:
The symbol of a purest nature.

Often, I stand wondering at you,
Enchanted by your makeup mere.
Does God forget to insert a soul in you?
Or do the souls forget to return from here?

Are you musing upon silently,
The songs sung in the heavenly cluster?
Wiggling in the morning wind softly,
Praising the greatness of your Master.

As the stars of the above skies shine,
You spread the splendour right here;
And in the little heart of mine,
A spring of joy, refreshing sheer.

28

Keep Believing

Keep Believing

Keep believing in yourself the first,
And in your special dreams the most
That they will come true on your way,
That you can do it, one day.

Because I believe in another dawn;
In a rising anew, a life – reborn.

The challenges and charges will change,
The troubles and toils will rearrange;
For I know that this time will go,
It will not be the same tomorrow.

Because I believe in another dawn;
In a rising anew, a life – reborn.

Clouds above the blues never stop to drift,
Autumn after winter never forgets to shift,
Sea waves never halt to plane the shore,
Then to be worried in life, not any more.

Because I believe in another dawn;
In a rising anew, a life – reborn.

29

An Angel from Above

An Angel from Above

If I could paint on a canvas your soul,
Only a captivating butterfly can resemble:
The matchless beauty that you possess,
The inseparable qualities you express;
As variegated colours arranged in unison,
The infinite shapes imprinted of a horizon.

As a butterfly sets her eyes on buds,
You seek in everything the goodness;
As a butterfly hurts not a single petal,
You meet everyone soft and gentle;
As a butterfly stir up the passionate mind,
You induce the beats of joyous kind.

I like more your silent fluttering,
And a hand's reach fervent flickering;
I relish ever your ardent company
As a child behind the incarnate symphony,
And I know you'll alight on me,
If I am silent and rapt on thee.

For, you are an angel sent from above
To pour out the liniment of love.

30
Time-Present

Time-Present

Time-present presents the 'future'
And grants the 'past' to mature.
Both co-exist in this very moment
Like, deflection of the same 'present'.

In the eternal present time flows
To and fro, as a pendulum moves.
Past as its vanishing shadow
And future, its glorious halo.

A present slipped is extravagant
If we know its value significant.
It's the gift, a heavenly promise
To make the finest, if you not miss.

It is the only assurance, the now
To live further and to grow above;
For the day past is for ever gone
And the day to come has not born.

Wake up! Behold this moment,
Let it not go without a present;
It is your own, but only the now
To partake you, in the Eternal Now.

31
An Equivalent Benefit

An Equivalent Benefit

Every unpleasant grief and pain,
Credit not misery or pass in vain;
A seed is hidden, of equivalent benefit.

Every mountain is gifted with
A delightful valley together with;
For a slope is inbuilt in every steep.

The dark clouds ever prevail not,
A clear sky, pleasant is to be sought;
Wind will blow to spread the blue again.

Night's deep will not creep so long,
A dawn awaits with morning song,
And the bright rays of truth to reign over.

Unless a seed decay inside the soil,
Letting to die beneath, facing the foil;
The life cannot sprout and the beginning.

Reach to the deeper than the profane,
Where the tears are sweet when restrain,
And add flavours of greater goodness.

32

To Beat the Song of Gratitude

To Beat the Song of Gratitude

Little have I given to the world,
After being received in train a hundredfold;
Life is written in the lines of debts-
Bestowed in every moment as gratuitous gifts.
A realization came about too late
That the span is too short to repay the fate;
For, the bounteous aids are countless,
Showered on my soul - always worthless.

Lord! I failed to see the greatness-
Of things around of use by everydayness;
I missed out to perceive the beauty
Of different seasons and their offspring lofty;
Often, I complained the days leaden,
And neglected the events and greatness hidden.

Lord! Give me the inner eye-
to see differently, the inherent goodness high;
Create a broad mind of acceptance
To share this world and all its magnificence;
And form a tender heart of flesh,
To beat the song of gratitude, unselfish.

33

I Need You Now

I Need You Now

It is as dark as a moonless night,
Without a ray of light to hope for.
Even in a bright day, I feel my plight,
As a retiring tide from its loving shore.

The dreadful silence to swallow and smear,
The fearful fantasies to crawl on thoughts;
The whirl-wind of rising suffering, I hear,
And the ugly laughter of hidden threats.

It is too heavy the heart, sorrow-sicken
Also, the body too delicate to bear.
Each moment strange, odd and raven,
Alone I am, with no one to share.

Thence, I turned towards you, my whole
When I realized, I lost you from within;
Left alone in barren wilderness my soul,
Craves you in the valley of agony deep in.

Lord, I need you now than ever more,
Your comforting hug and kiss of trust;
For with you I can walk miles more,
Pacific and tranquil against a tempest.

34

Graceful Living

Graceful Living

You have loved me into my being
That made the different seeing.
You awakened my heart from slumber
And set the rhythmic beat in number;
Elevated my soul from deadly numbness
And filled with vital positiveness.

To let me know what is the permanent,
You cut off the opulence transient;
To make me dauntless and daring,
You formed in the hearth of suffering;
To teach me the benefit of perseverance,
You permitted the trails and annoyance.

The real joy you showed in serving
And the greatest content in self-giving.
The light of true knowledge you offered,
To progress in spirit high treasured;
The right way revealed in your model
To reach me to the eternal citadel.

All to mould in me, a graceful living
For, you have loved me into my being.

35

Freedom ever be with You

Freedom ever be with You

Let the freedom ever be with you
To think free, act free, what is 'you'.
It's the substratum by you are formed
And the greatest wealth to be lived.

Freedom shape you human, the gift,
And make you victor of inner shift.
It is in your conviction, it lives,
And in your depravity, it starves.

When the tide of your wants rescind,
From the shores of the restless mind;
And the pleasant wind of content blows,
An inner realization of freedom flows.

When the fears and worries lay to rest,
In the valleys of the time past;
The days of hope and joy it begets,
To receive a world in the new outsets.

Then, your face would reflect its beads,
Words would beget its spirited seeds;
The deeds would define its concepts,
Your presence would proclaim the percepts.

36

Sacred Solitude

Sacred Solitude

'Ascend to a world of sacred solitude',
I heard my mind's call.
For it is the power in vast magnitude,
The rhythm divine in all.

Silence, the language of angels so sacred,
Of the mystical symbols;
And the music of nature harmoniously united
In love, the vibrant pulse.

In walls of silence, you came to this world,
And'll return in same silence.
The moments you could embrace her, behold!
To dissolve in the presence.

It becomes the medicine to heal all distresses,
The channel of heavenly graces;
And the greatest revealer, beyond appearances,
Of the eternal traces.

Silence is the treasure, all can confront:
The animate and the inanimate.
In mountain highs and deep trenches consistent,
Also as your inner self's associate.

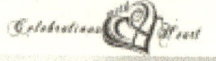

37

A Rapture on a Blade of Grass

A Rapture on a Blade of Grass

There is a rapture on every blade of grass-
Bathed in cool morning's misty mass.

The gift of a new dawn, pure and holy,
Twinkling in the sunshine sweet and silky.

Infinite colours of nature in unison-
In single drop, reflecting the morning sun.

The captivating beauty of magnificent nature,
Manifested fairly, in single miniature.

How wonderful and arcane its Creator-
To insert a world in a dinky drop would be.

As a human soul, the sheerest and simplest
And the spark of the Creator the Greatest.

Far mysterious to know all its faculties
Yet, the most revealed in one's activities.

To search a life without the soul is in vain
But within, the whole universe can gain.

For, it is formed in the image and likeness-
Of the Lord of the cosmos and its vastness.

38

Pain and Suffering

Pain and Suffering

Pain and suffering can never be a less good
But a blessing bestowed by Mother Nature.
A universal language as it to be understood,
Trimming and shaping to grow and nurture.

To form her sons more deeply rooted
As a tree on a high mountain range.
To mould you in all the settings suited
Against the storms, and the seasons strange.

It's a device to make you more humble;
To eliminate self-love and vain vanity,
To build a heart, soft and understandable,
To wipe the neighbour's tear with parity.

Pain will aglow the reason to assess;
To keep the record of past and its errors,
To rise from the falls and trespasses,
To born and to live the morrow's favours.

Suffering, the greatest teacher of all kind,
To bring the benefit right from the agony.
Lo! The greatest medicine for humankind,
Gain the strength to change you and destiny.

39

I Meet You Inside

I Meet You Inside

When I meet you deep inside,
I find all and everything;
I get the meaning for everything.

For I searched a shoulder for long:
To unload my worries distressful
And its chained shadows fretful.

That I wished, I could see a face:
To console my soul lonely,
To bring the joy within really.

Again I waited to find a hand:
To hold me close in its warmth,
To feel the heed in all its depth.

And I dreamt I could rise again,
Regardless of the broken wings
Above the wants, though it clings.

When I meet you deep inside,
I find all and everything;
I get the meaning for everything.

40
The Day is not Far

The Day is not Far

When the days adore you a king and greet,
You feel the world under your feet.

The possessions seat you on the throne of fame,
Men and might together praise your name.

You know only a world glittering and prodigal,
But remain stranger to its hardness and struggle.

You enjoy the comforts and safety of garments,
Being unknown to the plight of the pavements.

If you know or not, the couch of currencies even
Is sufficient not to buy a night's sleep fasten.

And even a train of gold and precious stones,
Also not enough to bring the true happiness.

Behold! The day is not far, to come in your life
To shake you, as the west wind on withered leaf.

The sound of laughter you'll hear on street's soil,
And will wonder at content faces after a day's toil.

Thence, you will leave the palace as Siddhartha,
The first step to light, to become Buddha.

41

To Sail Beyond the Sunset

To Sail Beyond the Sunset

To sail beyond the sunset,
You need inside the fire, unrest;
To lighten the dreary perception,
Until the farthest destination.

Waves may raise a mountain high,
And a storm may divert your eye;
In the whirl wind of irregular tide,
Your journey can recklessly slide.

The darkness may choke your sight
And you may be left alone in plight;
The long awaited dawn may late,
And you may be lost in deep fate.

Yet, my friend, keep faith in you–
The inner-being's power to rescue;
For, it is the source of unfailing fuel
And can be trusted without a dual.

The one who hears the inner call,
And its vibrant beat in the soul–
Would stand on the trials uncertain,
In the voyage to the other shore certain.

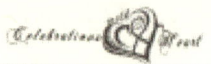

42

Roses of a Shy November

Roses of a Shy November

The late roses of a shy November
With soft, early morning dews;
Hesitated, to leave the slumber
And their more solemn muse.

"Why are you blooming not yet"?
The bees sue for, waiting so long;
"Let the sun shine more bright",
Retorted the buds all along.

But, the hillside breeze ever soothing,
Brought forth the chill, surprising;
And moved on further announcing
"The winter is fast approaching".

It's a time to shed the stature,
To leave the likings and colours,
To stand humbled, before Nature-
The giver and taker of all favours.

Mind to bloom without a diffidence,
The time is too precious and limited.
A spring or winter, the assurance-
Is the fragrance that to be emitted.

43

A Search for Identity

A Search for Identity

Life! An unending search for identity,
From birth till death in uniformity.
"Who am I?" A seven thousand times
Changing and changing as gambling games;
Sometimes anxious and sometimes confident,
Again sometimes worried as a defendant;
Other times as a great combatant,
An incessant struggle against systems existent.
Often, I found in the hands of the Lord favourite,
Dissolved in the silence as an anchorite;
But there are times lost in the loneliness,
And crave for a ray of light in the darkness.
Created as a little less than angel,
And still behaves as an animal.
Life as a twirling between the steeps and slopes,
Or squeezed in the rift of extreme deeps.
Joys and sorrows or laughter and tears,
As two sides of a coin, success and failures.

Countless 'I' and their unfolding imageries,
As the varied seasons and myriad sceneries.
Yet, this unbroken change and unending motion,
Constitute the identity towards the Eternal notion.

44

The Breezeless Summer Night

The Breezeless Summer Night

The heavy breezeless summer night dragging,
Where all leaves stand still and meditating;
The time creeps and craws much hesitated,
Even the sleep to embrace is so long halted.

The sounds of night daunt than darkness:
The whistling of crickets pierces the stillness,
The owlet's cry echoes in the surrounding,
And the more to frighten wild canines' howling.

The dark mid-hours to hover the lifeless shadows,
And to brood the buried images of past sorrows.
As the fired clouds swift all in random,
And heat the inner core in high momentum.

Those promises which I failed to surrender,
Memories which I do not like to remember,
The duties, which are neglected and forgotten;
But, ascend anew as ghosts of forsaken.

The rays of a new dawn caressed vehemently
And vanished the bogeys as shades derelictly.
But left a full day vital, before my stature
To fulfil the past and to prepare the future.

45

In the Company of Nature

In the Company of Nature

I love not to be with the men the less
But in the company of nature the more;
For the totality that ever encompasses
The rhythm divine in all to adore.

The music that connects all inhabitants
The beat of life to share as a whole;
The homogeneity kept up with ferments
The balance in movements in one and all.

The blue sky over the heads is same
And the air to refresh the inner soul;
The brightened day and moonlit frame,
Green trees and milky clouds is for all.

The life events partake in the becoming,
Continuous change constitutes an identity
Pain or happiness, failing or succeeding,
The moments are harmonious in cosmicity.

The manifold modes, the cells of universe,
As the waves rise and dissolve in one unity;
As a molten flux the face of nature evolves
Yet, beyond the reach remain the veracity.

46
The Bond of Life

The Bond of Life

I know your heart,
That your smile means much more
Than to converse a simple good-bye;
But a poem recited by heart,
Where the dreams ascend on wings
And their words as a flowing river;
Yet, lingering to come out to my reach:
The joys you wanted to share
And the sorrows hid within,
As a silent cry – a waterless fall.
I feel your silence,
As the moon experience amidst thousand stars:
The deep feelings
And mixed sentiments,
That you covered by a laboured smile;
A vain effort to subdue any
As the clouds to check morning rays.

But my dear friend,
The pain of farewell is sweeter than honey
Though is thicker than a night in woods;
And even the distance or time never can whittle
The strongest bond of life – Friendship.

47
The Most Precious Given

The Most Precious Given

Time, the most precious given
But the least cared and driven;
As the endless sky's free raven,
Flits away from one' own stretch.

Time inbuilt and very much near
In the very being, as eternal gear;
To lose a bit of it, the greatest fear
For every loss adds incompleteness.

Time brings a range of possibility,
For every man with will of credibility,
To use one's own power of creativity,
To form oneself - a better human.

Time is the fuel of life's mechanism,
For all activities, a basic substratum:
To present with modes of reformism
To ascend the rungs of life's success.

Time passed is departed for ever;
Life is lost by moments cared never.
If the time given for a being is over,
The world calls ruthlessly – The Dead.

48
Solemn Loneliness

Solemn Loneliness

Thoughts of thick seclusions,
Deeper than the woods of the Southern range
Intense and intimate, random and strange.

The aching void often enchant,
The past moments and sweet memories
As resonance heard from the distant valleys.

In the night's darkened dread,
The tender feelings lose the flavour and freeze
As the naked branches before mountain breeze.

Only the solitary musings befriend,
Where the silence is heavy and brooding over
As in a nightmare, the surroundings hover.

The unfulfilled desires heap over,
On the deep planes of mind's inwardness
As the dead leaves patter in the wilderness.

Yet, I enjoy solemn loneliness,
For I find myself immersed in the wholeness
Of the past, present and future, in this vastness.

49

A Breeze can Sing More

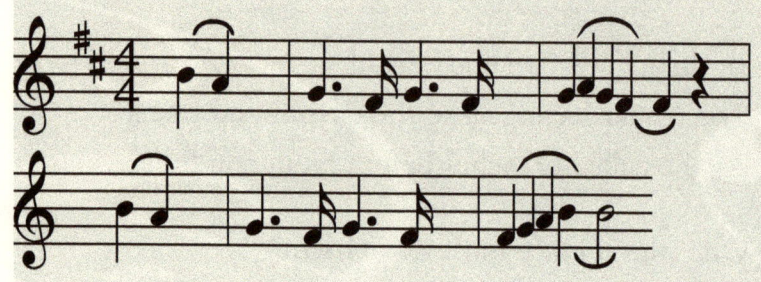

A Breeze can Sing More

I failed to know that ever before,
A breeze can sing melodious more.

Sweeter than a flute, sharper than harp,
Soothing and pleasing o'er human grasp.

The music of nature where all can dissolve,
The rhythm divine where all resolve.

As lullaby sent by Mother Nature,
Consoling and comforting every creature.

So gentle, but heard by delicate weeds;
So emollient, yet felt by tender breeds.

Intense in the valleys that echoing heavy,
Frightening in the woods thick and hefty.

Flies and kites to dance the rhythmic notes,
Buds and twigs to frisk in refreshing beats.

Composed of deep feelings where it blows,
A warm day or cool night together flows.

Embraces the rich or poor all alike,
And heel the wounds of past to make.

Awakes the memories hidden and faded,
To relive life's pleasant memories heeded.

50

Life is to Advance

Life is to Advance

Nothing more joyous than a weary day,
Sweater than the sweat of a hard way;
For, every dream has a toil to accomplish,
As every pearl has its course to furnish.

The call of duty is high and demanding,
Inbuilt in the very image of one's being;
For no one is ever born without a role,
To fulfil in life-time, unique and sole.

The act of work equals a sacred worship,
To partake humans in God's craftsmanship;
As an unfinished project, everyone is created
And the call to form oneself is to be realized.

The real achievement is in fulfilling duty,
And the satisfaction, the way of activity.
The joy is not fleeting, fruit is everlasting,
It is a gift given to mankind in becoming.

So, life is to advance, a strive to advance-
To the fullness, a life long performance;
And the hard work is the cost of perfection,
As the labour pain for a new creation.

I feel for You

www.ingramcontent.com/pod-product-compliance
Lightning Source LLC
Chambersburg PA
CBHW032129090426
42743CB00007B/526